Texas History
Writing Prompts

Written by Laurie Cockerell

Kinderfable Press
Fort Worth, Texas

Dedication

For Buggee and Mom
-LC

Book Design by Laurie Cockerell
Editor: Yvonne Cumberland

Kinderfable Press
P.O. Box 10193
Fort Worth, Texas 76114
www.kinderfablepress.com

ISBN: 978-0-9845609-6-7

Printed in the United States of America

Imagine Texas

Most teachers agree their students best retain knowledge when actively engaged in some personal way. Classroom lectures and storybooks impart information, but when students participate in the lesson through activities, the result is better comprehension and memory retention.

Imagine Texas provides intriguing writing prompts and activities for your Texas history student. Various writing techniques and skills are offered to give your students practice in not only putting their thoughts and stories into words, but also understanding and remembering Texas's amazing and unforgettable history.

If you and your students enjoy these exercises, we urge you to consider the three-book *Spirit of Texas* history curriculum (written by the author, Laurie Cockerell, and Yvonne Cumberland) as a supplement to your Texas history and writing studies.

This curriculum is available at:
www.kinderfablepress.com, amazon, and Teachers Pay Teachers.

Photograph and image credits may be found at the end of the book.

Table of Contents

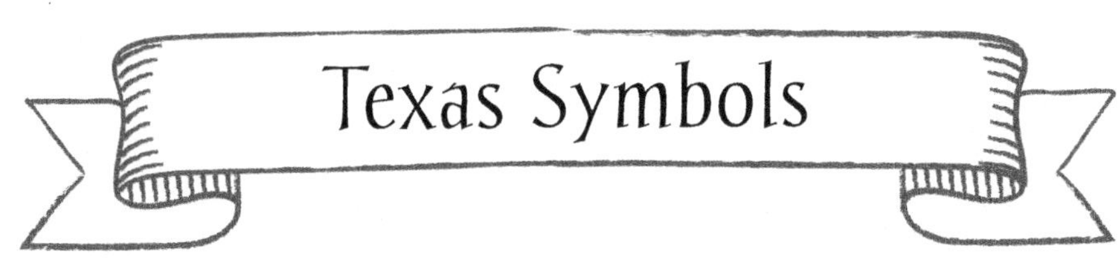

Bluebonnets

Texans love bluebonnets! They bloom in the spring, filling fields and lining roadsides throughout the state. The bluebonnet (also known as *Lupinus subcarnosus*) is the official Texas state flower, designated by the Texas legislature in 1901.

There are several myths told about the origin of the bluebonnet. Now it is your turn to add to the lore about the source of this lovely flower. Write a story entitled "How the Bluebonnet Came to Be." Feel free to include magic and mythical beings, if you'd like. Tell a tale both children and adults will enjoy. Be creative!

Six Flags Over Texas

Six different national flags have flown over Texas at one time or another during the last five hundred years.

Imagine:

What if history changed?
What if any one of the first five countries
(Spain, France, Mexico, the Republic of Texas, or the Confederate States of America)
still governed Texas?
How would our lives, culture, language, and government be different?
Write five short paragraphs. Each paragraph should describe your perception of what Texas would look like if it remained under the rule of that particular country today.

The official state bird of Texas is the mockingbird! It can imitate the songs and sounds of many different types of birds, as well as other animals.

Write a humorous story about a mockingbird who mimics another animal, resulting in confusion and a funny outcome.

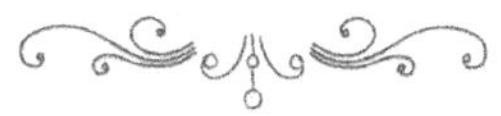

Texas Regions

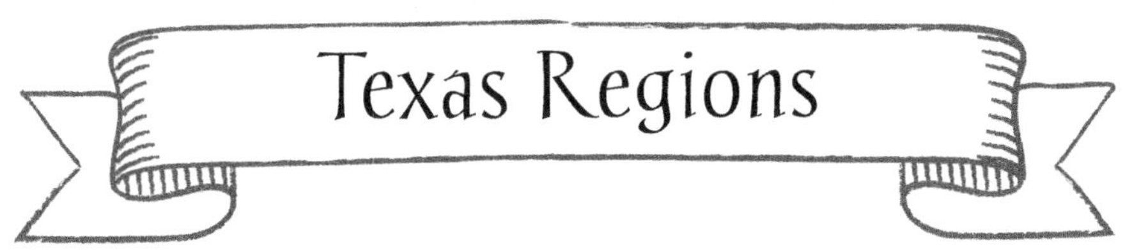

A state as big as Texas has seven very diverse and fascinating regions. From tall pine trees to sandy beaches to canyons and flat, treeless plains ...Texas has the perfect vacation spot for everyone.

Imagine:

You have been asked to write a three-sentence, five-star review of each region. Think of a short and accurate description for each region, along with a list of your favorite local sites and things to do. Even if you haven't actually visited the areas, do a little research and make plans for your next vacation!

Prairies and Lakes

Piney Woods

Gulf Coast Plains

South Texas Plains
Hill Country
Big Bend
Panhandle Plains

The Tale of a Lightning Whelk

The lightning whelk was adopted as the official Texas state shell in 1987. This particular spiraling shell is unusual because the opening is on the left side of the shell and the whorls coil in a counter-clockwise direction. In fact, the scientific name of this shell is *Busycon perversum pulleyi*: the word *perversum* means "turned the wrong way." The object you see to the lower left of the shell is a lightning whelk egg case. It can contain up to 200 eggs!

Unless you are an early riser, it's difficult to find one of these treasures. Every morning collectors search for shells like this on Texas beaches, hoping to add to their cache. Write a story about a lightning whelk snatched up by a beachcomber early one morning in Galveston. Who finds it? Where do they carry it as they continue their walk? Where do they keep it when they get home? Add to your plot by having the shell passed along to three more people. How did the other owners come to possess the shell?

Native Americans

The buffalo was the center of many Native Americans' lives. These magnificent beasts were the source of food, shelter, clothing, tools, weapons, and other necessary items. Many Texas Indians regularly picked up their homes and moved across miles and miles of prairie land, just to follow the buffalo.

Imagine:

You are a young Texas Indian brave. You are finally old enough to join a buffalo hunt. It's an exciting—and somewhat frightening—day for you! Returning after a successful hunt, you sit around a fire and tell the younger children about your day. Be sure to share all the details of the hunt in first person. Since it's your first hunt and you are talking to younger kids, feel free to exaggerate a little. After all, a young person in this situation might be prone to using a little hyperbole!

Hyperbole: an exaggerated claim that should not be taken literally.

Misunderstood Karankawa!

The Karankawa were one of Texas's most fascinating tribes! Sometimes friendly, sometimes fierce, probably smelly from their alligator grease mosquito repellent, and even occasionally practicing cannibalism ... this tribe also served as one of our state's first greeting committees and hosts to the earliest European explorers.

Imagine:

You are a loyal Karankawa tribal member. A brave (but nervous!) newspaper reporter pays a visit to Galveston Island. He wants to give you a chance to help explorers and settlers better understand you and your customs. It's time to set the record straight!

Record the complete interview as printed in the local newspaper. Add the reporter's final perception of the Karankawa after hearing your side of the story.

Three Sisters

The planting and harvest of corn, beans, and squash was common among many farming Native American tribes. This trio of vegetables was known as the "Three Sisters." First, corn was planted under a small pile of dirt; bean and squash seeds were then planted next to the corn. As the corn grew tall, the beans climbed up the corn stalk, which supported the bean vines. The squash vines spread on the ground around the bottom of these plants, protecting the soil from weeds and erosion. Today we call this type of farming practice "companion planting."

There are many mythical legends about the origin of the name "Three Sisters." Write your own legend. Who were the sisters? And why was this type of planting given that particular name? Be original!

Texas Explorers

It seemed as if the Spanish Narváez expedition was doomed. First, soldiers were accidentally separated from their ships, stranded in Florida with unhappy Native Americans who were anxious for the conquistadors to leave. After building rafts and sailing along the Gulf Coast, the Spaniards encountered a storm near Galveston and became castaways on the beach. Soon after, they were made captives of local Native Americans. The few remaining survivors eventually escaped and made their way to safety in Mexico.

Imagine:

Cell phones are magically available and the conquistadors of the 1500s are able to send text messages. Pretend you are Cabeza de Vaca and you can charge your cell phone on sunshine alone. Create a series of texts as you converse with your best friend back home in Spain, from the time of your shipwreck in Texas through the completion of your journey to Mexico.

Fransisco Vázquez de Coronado

Remember Coronado's expedition in 1540? Just like the Narváez expedition, things just didn't work out as planned. This huge caravan of soldiers, friendly Indians, servants, and animals set out on a journey with the hope of finding cities rumored to be filled with gold, silver, and turquoise. Instead, they experienced battles with Native Americans and a tricky man named "El Turko," who led the explorers on a wild goose chase. They returned to Mexico with empty pockets, and the journey was considered a failure.

Imagine:

What if the expedition had, in fact, been successful? What if the explorers discovered the seven cities of gold and returned home heroes? Retell the story of the Coronado expedition, but with an alternate ending. Don't forget to add how a different outcome might have changed history in more ways than one!

La Salle's Lament

Poor Monsieur La Salle! His voyage to the New World and his plan to colonize and create a port at the mouth of the Mississippi River was a disaster. One ship lost to pirates ... then La Salle lost his way and landed at Matagorda Bay, Texas, instead of Louisiana ... one ship turned back ... two ships and supplies destroyed ... unhappy Karankawa neighbors ... miserable French soldiers and terrible illness resulted in a failed expedition and colony.

Create a first-person rap or poem La Salle might have written, lamenting his bad luck and unsuccessful voyage.

Keeping the French at Bay

Although Spain seemed to have lost interest in Texas, their interest returned when they learned of La Salle's failed French colony. Something must be done to protect their land from outsiders! While explorer Alonso de León and others supported the creation of a system of missions to help populate the land, surely others considered different methods to bring new citizens to the territory and protect this important asset.

Imagine:

You have been selected to serve on a committee with Mr. De León and others. This committee has been assigned the job of generating suggestions to deter the French from further attempts at colonizing Texas. Committees usually begin their task by brainstorming ideas. Pretend you are serving as secretary for the group, and write notes including each member's suggestion. Record all of the ideas, how long they will take, how expensive it will be for Spain to finance the plans, problems that might arise, and anything else critical to consider with each proposal.

La Salle's ships at the entrance of Matagorda Bay.

Missions & Presidios

Missions were built for several reasons: to settle and colonize an unexplored country, to spread Christianity and Catholicism, and to educate Native Americans and immerse them in the Spanish culture. Of course, Spain also hoped the presence of missions and presidios would discourage the French from once again trespassing on Texas soil. Missions provided a place of safety from tribal enemies and a more constant food supply, while presidios were forts built to help protect the missions and settlements which would grow nearby.

Using each letter from the words "Mission" and "Presidio," create two acrostic poems. The first word of each line should begin with the letter to the left of the line. Hint: the word "protect" might be a good suggestion for the first letter in "presidio."

M ______________________

I ______________________

S ______________________

S ______________________

I ______________________

O ______________________

N ______________________

P ______________________

R ______________________

E ______________________

S ______________________

I ______________________

D ______________________

I ______________________

O ______________________

LIFE IN THE MISSION

While not all Native Americans chose to participate and live at the missions, some did find safety, education, and a new religion within the walls. Those who chose to stay were trained in skills such as carpentry, blacksmithing, weaving, raising livestock, and more.

Imagine:

You are a young Native American boy or girl, and your family has chosen to live within one of the Texas missions. Your best friend, whose family decided not to leave their tribal home, climbs over the wall one day and asks how you like living at the mission. Do you feel safe? Are you scared and confused? Are you learning new things and making friends? Do you miss your old life? Using dialogue only, share this conversation with your best friend, helping him/her understand your new life and how you feel about the change your family has made.

Missions ... Possible!

The most famous of all the Texas missions is the Alamo. Almost every Texan has heard about the Alamo and has likely even toured the mission chapel on a family trip to San Antonio. The familiar shape of the building and the story of the battle that took place there is known throughout the world.

But do you know about the other missions located throughout the state? Over thirty missions were built in Texas between 1682-1793. They all eventually closed, but some of them and their chapels still remain. You can visit five of these missions in San Antonio; each one has a different look and personality.

Pick one of the San Antonio missions and write an informative/expository essay about that mission. Be sure to include the dates of operation, the origin of the mission's name, where the mission is located, a description of the architecture, and whether or not the mission you can visit today is the original structure or partially reconstructed and why.

Filibusters

A cannon, a petticoat, and a hammock. What do these three items have in common? They were all used for survival by Jane Long, as she awaited her husband James' return to Bolivar Island in 1821. The leader of a filibustering expedition, James had been captured and imprisoned in Mexico City. Sadly, Jane would never see James again. However, to trick the local Karankawa Indians into believing there were still soldiers at the fort, she flew a red petticoat like a flag and fired a cannon every day. Jane also fished in the gulf using a hammock as a net so she and her children would not starve. Jane, also known as "The Mother of Texas," was quite a survivor!

Now it's your turn:

Write another survival story using these same three items, but set your story in a different time and place. Don't use the items in the same way. Be creative and tell a NEW survival story!

A Filibuster and a Hook

As many Mexican citizens began to be unhappy with Spanish rule, a significant filibuster took place in Texas between 1812-1813. Two men, Jose Gutiérrez de Lara and Augustus Magee, gathered an army (named the Republican Army) and invaded Texas with hopes of taking the land from Spain and starting their own country. After capturing the city of Nacogdoches, the expedition marched into San Antonio and declared the land free from Spain. Of course, Spain was not willing to give up that easily. They sent Colonel Joaquín de Arredondo to fight the filibusters. Arredondo and his Spanish soldiers overwhelmed the filibusters at the Battle of Medina, once again recovering control of San Antonio. Colonel Arredondo was known to be a cruel leader and showed no mercy. Training at his side was a young soldier Texans would later come to fear: Santa Anna!

It is important to begin your writing with a hook. Engage your reader from the very beginning of your story so he/she wants to keep reading and find out what happens next. You can use several techniques:

- *use a sound (onomatopoeia) to grab their attention.*
- *open your story with a riddle, a bit of humor, or a question for the reader.*
- *start with a famous quotation or a short dialogue.*

Retell the story of the Gutiérrez-Magee Expedition and the Battle of Medina in your own words, but open your story with a hook which will make your reader think, "I can't wait to see what is going to happen!"

A Roll of the Dice

Spanish authorities were suspicious of a man named Philip Nolan. He illegally captured horses in Texas and sold them to buyers in the United States. In 1800, Nolan led twenty-eight armed men into Texas and set up corrals near the Brazos River, where the men captured and penned wild horses. One day, Spanish soldiers surprised Nolan and his men and began to fight. Nolan was killed, and the surviving horse thieves were taken to a Mexican prison. The Spanish king insisted one of the nine prisoners be put to death. The men rolled dice from a crystal cup onto a drum, and the unlucky prisoner who threw the lowest number was hanged.

The rolling of dice is often associated with taking some type of risk. Make a list of ten risks you would be willing to take. Then think of ten risks you would NOT be willing to take. Explain whether the reward would be worth the risk in each case ... or not?

A Chance Encounter

Serendipity. Have you ever heard the term?

In 1820, two acquaintances happened to see each other as they walked down a street in San Antonio. A disappointed Moses Austin had just returned from an unsuccessful meeting with Spanish government officials. He had hoped to gain Spain's approval for his "empresario" plan to bring new colonists to Texas from the United States. Although they had only met once many years ago, Baron de Bastrop and Moses Austin locked eyes as they passed by and recognized each other. *Serendipity*! Baron de Bastrop offered to introduce Austin and help him convince government officials his idea would be beneficial to both Spain and the colonists. His offer was ultimately successful, and the rest is history!

Imagine:

What if Moses Austin had NOT looked up and seen Baron de Bastrop? What if his empresario plan had never been approved? Consider how the history of Texas would be different. Then write a journal entry for today, as yourself. Your entry should be about a normal day in your life, assuming Moses Austin and Baron de Bastrop had never looked up and recognized each other on that fortuitous day in 1820. Without Austin's empresario system, it's possible Texas would have never gained independence from Mexico. Make sure your reader can "read between the lines" and recognize how our state might not be what it is today had this serendipitous event never occurred.

Moses Austin

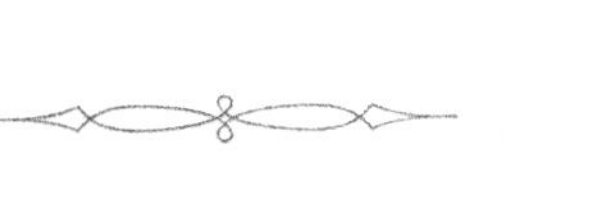

Baron de Bastrop

Empresarios

Soon after Moses Austin's empresario plan was approved, he became ill and died. Fortunately, his son Stephen agreed to carry out his father's arrangement to bring new colonists to Texas from the United States. Stephen knew it was important he only accept settlers with a good reputation and background. In fact, he said, "Drunkards, gamblers, swearers, and idlers need not apply!"

Imagine:

You, Stephen F. Austin, are interviewing two potential colonists. One of the colonists is a perfect citizen, just the type of man (or woman) you plan to select. The other is a real stinker—just the type you would reject. Using dialogue and the same questions for each colonist, describe the interviews you conduct with your potential settlers. Since you are writing only dialogue, record your thoughts within the dialogue, using italics to help your reader imagine how the hopeful colonists look and sound to Mr. Austin.

Dog and Possum Trot

Many cabins built during the 1800s looked like the home pictured here. These dogtrot houses (also known as breezeway or possom-trot cabins) were built with a big hole in the middle! This breezeway allowed air to flow through the middle of the house, cooling it off on warm and sticky summer days.

Imagine:

You live in a dogtrot house, right on the Brazos River. Your family built the cabin by hand. Imagine you've just awakened. It's early in the morning and you step into the breezeway to watch the sunrise. Write about this experience with a focus on atmosphere. Don't write dialogue. Just describe what you see. What you feel. What you hear. What you smell. Use beautiful language to make your reader smile and wish they could be standing there with you.

Almost every Texan has heard the famous story of the Battle of Gonzales and the *Come and Take It* cannon. In October of 1835, Mexican soldados marched to Gonzales with orders to retrieve a small cannon, but local citizens refused to turn it over. Instead, Texians met the soldados on the banks of the Guadalupe River with that cannon, a black and white flag embroidered with the words "Come and Take It" waving overhead. A short battle followed, with the soldados retreating and the Texians celebrating a win at the first battle of the Texas Revolution.

Wouldn't this story make a great movie?
You have been hired to produce and direct a movie about the Battle of Gonzales.
As director, you need to cast the movie, decide where to shoot the movie, and write a short script.
Include dialogue and stage directions.
Who knows? ...
Maybe you will actually direct this blockbuster film some day!

Texas Revolution

An elegy is a poem written about a sad or serious event, often a lament for the dead.

Write an elegy to express the sorrow felt in 1836, and even today, about the battle and fall of the Alamo.

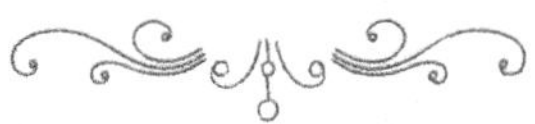

A Risky Declaration!

Delegates met at Washington-on-the-Brazos to declare Texas independence and write a new constitution in March of 1836. These were very brave men. They knew Santa Anna would consider them traitors, and it was clear the Mexican general was not a man to show mercy on those he considered treasonous.

"Would You Rather?" is a popular game. Consider these "Would You Rather" dilemmas from the standpoint of a delegate at the Convention of 1836. Decide which alternative you prefer and write one short paragraph for each question. Analyze the risks versus the consequences, and explain your choices.

Would You Rather?

1. Stay in Texas and risk Santa Anna's wrath ... or run away and hide in another state until the revolution is over?

2. If Texas wins the revolution, would you rather immediately join the United States ... or become a Republic and govern your own country?

3. Race to help the Texians at the Alamo (William Barret Travis just sent a letter informing the convention of their dire situation) ... or finish writing the new constitution and gather more help for General Houston?

4. Surrender to Santa Anna ... or keep on fighting, regardless of the odds?

General Profiles

In 1836, communication across the country ... across a state ... even across town, was slow and required quill and paper or a great deal of walking. Almost everything people knew about their leaders or current events was delivered through word of mouth or written words, and the news was possibly weeks old before reaching the receiver.

Imagine:

Social Media is alive and well in 1836! Wouldn't it have been interesting to know something more about the thoughts and personalities of the leaders of Texas and Mexico during the Texas Revolution? Create a social media profile for both the Texan and Mexican generals. What would each want you to know about them?

texasbook

Sam Houston

Education:

Works at:

From:

Marital Status:

Sam Houston shared a post:

Like Comment Share

Friends

Sam Houston shared a post:

Like Comment Share

Do you think Sam Houston and Santa Anna would have been social media friends?
Would they have "unfriended" or "blocked" the other once the revolution began? Why or why not?

t **texasbook**

Santa Anna

Education:

Works at:

From:

Marital Status:

Santa Anna shared a post:

Like Comment Share

Friends

Santa Anna shared a post:

Like Comment Share

"A man, more brave and honest, never lived ..."

Erastus (Deaf) Smith served as a scout for Stephen F. Austin and General Houston during the revolution and later led a company of Texas Rangers. He suffered a loss of hearing after a childhood illness, earning him the nickname "Deaf." This disability didn't slow him down though! After his death, Sam Houston wrote: "A man, more brave and honest, never lived."

What would life be like without one of your senses? Think about it. Then write: If you had to give up one of your senses, which would it be? Which sense would you least like to give up? What would you miss by losing a sense? What might you gain? Would your other senses be heightened? How would your life be different?

Runaway Scrape

Shortly after the Battle of the Alamo, Santa Anna and his army began to chase the remaining Texian soldiers and fleeing colonists across Texas. It was a frightening experience for those who had to leave their homes and possessions as they attempted to evade a very angry Santa Anna. The weather was cold and wet. The trail was muddy and dangerous. General Houston used this time of retreat to better train his small army and gather more supplies and men. Finally, better prepared, Sam Houston turned his soldiers toward Santa Anna and a remarkable battle was fought and won by the Texian Army.

Have you heard the term "plot twist?" It is a technique used by a writer to introduce a surprising change in the direction or outcome of a story. Many natural plot twists occurred during the Texas Revolution. Write a short story about this time period, using at least four plot twists. Surprise your reader!

The Sam Houston Oak near Gonzales, Texas: First stop for General Houston's troops and Gonzales refugees during the Runaway Scrape.

San Jacinto

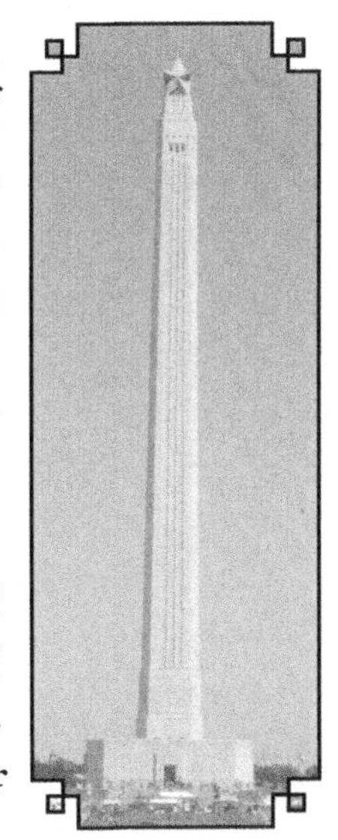

It seemed impossible. Thousands of highly trained Mexican soldiers versus Sam Houston's small ragtag army of Texians with little training and only a small supply of weapons and ammunition. But General Houston would not give up. Santa Anna and his soldados chased him across Texas as Houston slowly gathered the soldiers and supplies needed to turn and face the man who wanted to sweep Texas clean of the people he considered traitors to Mexico. On April 21st, the Texian army was ready. They defeated the Mexican Army in a short eighteen-minute battle known as the Battle of San Jacinto.

In fact, this was such an amazing feat ... maybe someone should write a manual entitled "How to Win a Revolution." You are the author of this manual! Using General Houston's techniques, help future leaders understand how to surprise the world by winning a battle and war, forever changing the future of a homeland and the lives of its citizens.

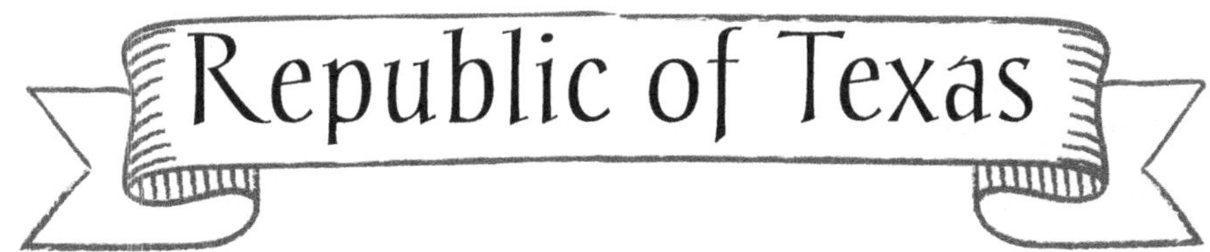

The Republic of Texas was led by three presidents: Sam Houston (served twice as president), Mirabeau Lamar, and Dr. Anson Jones. These three men were very different, and it was no secret Houston and Lamar disagreed on many issues. Treatment of Texas Native Americans, the Republic's debt and spending, and expansion of the military were just a few topics on which the two men did not see eye to eye.

Imagine:

Social Media is available during the time of the Republic! Write a "tweet" by President Lamar and a responding "tweet" by President Houston. Remember, you can only use up to 280 characters, and don't forget to end your tweet with a hashtag! #texasrocks!

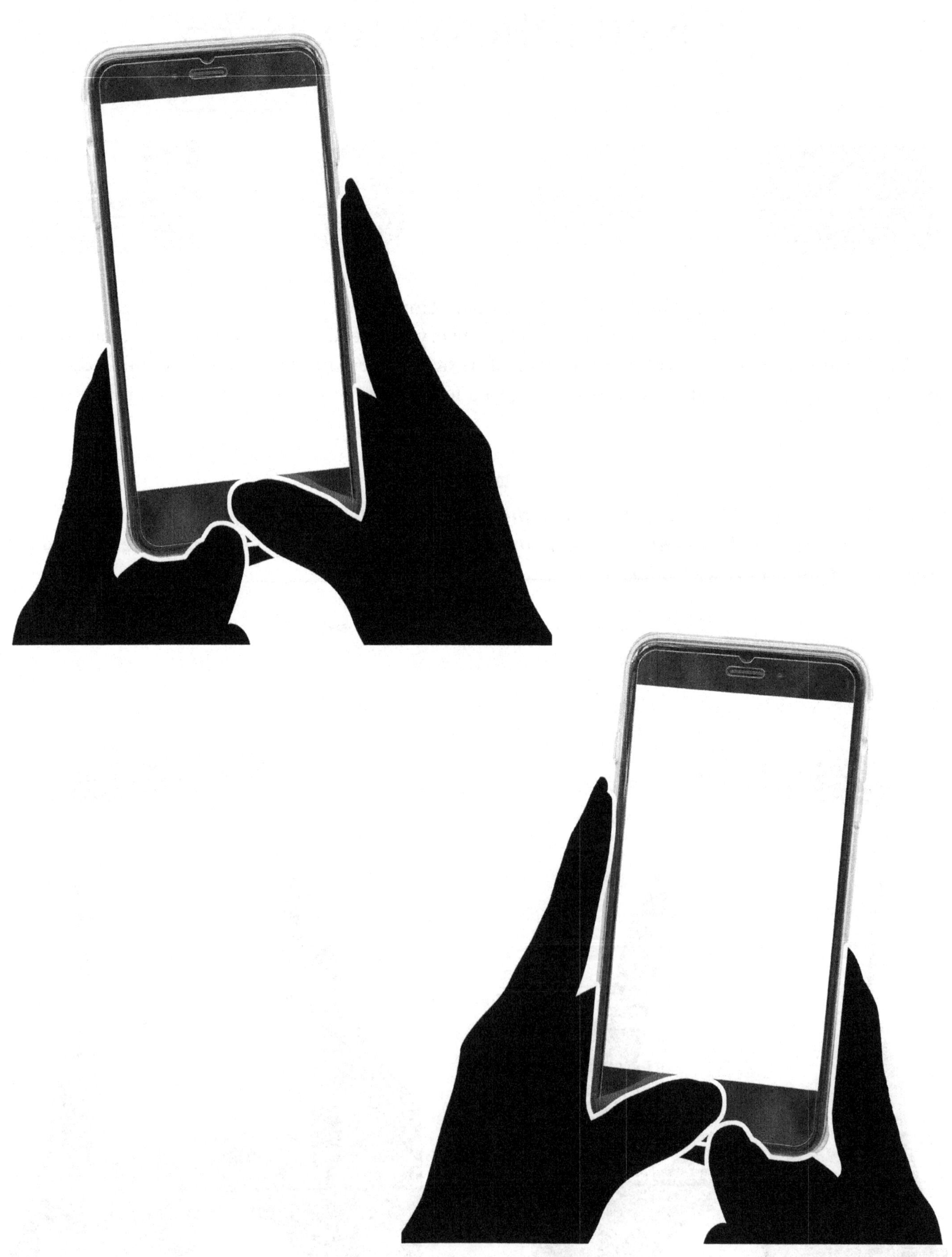

IMMIGRANTS

Many individuals and families began immigrating to Texas from the United States during the days of the empresario system. After Texas became a republic and later a state, folks also made their way to Texas from Europe. If you've ever visited Fredericksburg, then you've probably noticed the German culture's influence throughout the town. You'll see the French influence near San Antonio, and of course the culture, foods, and language of Mexico are found all over Texas. People braved risky ocean travel from Sweden, Switzerland, Norway, and other European countries. Texas still continues to attract new citizens from all over the world.

Imagine:

You live in Germany in 1842 and would like to make Texas your new home. Your parents have no desire to move, much less pack up everything they own to travel to some dangerous new country where people don't even speak their language! Write a persuasive letter to your parents. Convince them Texas is the perfect place to start on a fresh new adventure and make a home for your future children and grandchildren.

Angelina Eberly and the Archives War

Angelina Eberly was one tough cookie! Mexican soldados were once again threatening Texas, occupying San Antonio for a short time in 1842. President Houston worried the state archives Mirabeau Lamar had moved to Austin were in danger, so he sent rangers to retrieve the archives and bring them to Washington-on-the-Brazos. Mrs Eberly expressed her disapproval by shooting a cannon at the men leaving town with these important papers. She and her fellow Austin citizens were successful, and the archives were returned and remained in the state capital.

Plenty of songs have been written about strong women. Think of at least five existing song titles you might select which remind you of Angelina and her personality. Then think of five more song titles that reflect how the retreating men sent to bring the archives to President Houston must have felt after the failure of their mission.

Black Beans and Bad Luck

During President Houston's second term, about three hundred Texans went against orders and marched across the Rio Grande to attack Mier, Mexico, in 1843. After they were captured by the Mexican Army, Santa Anna ordered the execution of every tenth prisoner (17 out of the 176 men). Each man drew a bean from a jar to determine his fate. If the bean he selected was black, the soldier was executed; if it was white, he would be sent to prison instead. The survivors who chose a white bean either died in prison, escaped, or were eventually released. This sad story is known as "The Black Bean Episode."

Imagine:

You are one of the lucky survivors who drew a white bean. Write a formal letter to Texas authorities, who have asked for an official account of the international drama. Relate the story of your capture, the Black Bean Episode, and your escape or release. Focus not only on the events, but on your thoughts, emotions, and reactions to each experience.

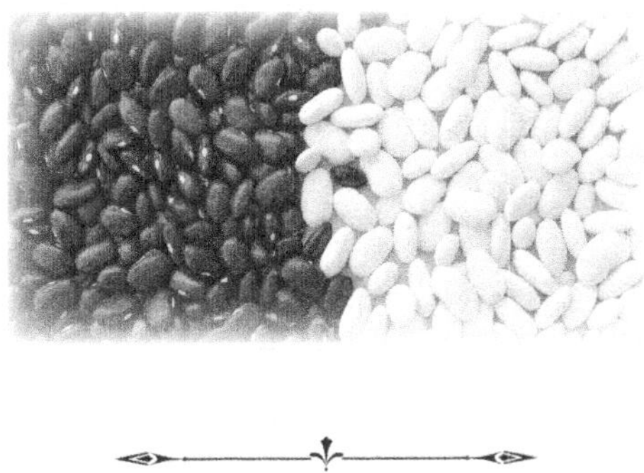

Statehood

Does December 25th ring a bell? October 31st? January 1st? July 4th?

Sure they do! But does the date December 29th mean anything to you? It should! That's the day (in 1845) Texas officially became the 28th state to join the Union. On February 19th, 1846, the Republic's President Anson Jones turned his office over to the newly-elected state governor, James Pinckney Henderson. The Lone Star flag was lowered and the Stars and Stripes took its place.

Don't you think one of these important dates deserves its own holiday? Pick either December 29th or February 19th as a new official state holiday. What name would you give the holiday? How should we celebrate? Should schools be closed that day? What special foods should we eat and songs should we sing? Do we wear costumes? Decorate? Design Texas's newest holiday and make it fun!

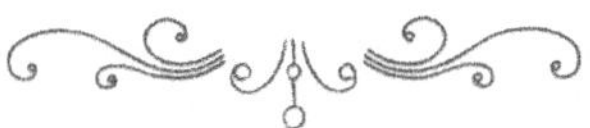

The picture above shows President Anson Jones and the annexation ceremony, February 19, 1846.

Texas Rangers!

The Texas Rangers were, and still are, a brave lot! They have faced danger since the early days of Texas colonization. Legend has it the phrase, "One Riot, One Ranger," derives from the story of an illegal prize fight which was to take place in Dallas. The Dallas mayor met Texas Ranger Captain Bill McDonald at the train station and asked Captain McDonald when the other rangers were coming. Captain McDonald replied, "Ain't I enough?"

Write a fictional story about one amazing, brave Texas Ranger, who single-handedly saves the day in a very perilous situation.

What? No Hollywood?

Texas only "thought" their troubles were over with Mexico after the revolution and annexation. However another war was to come: this time, the Mexican-American War. And *this* time the war was between Mexico and the United States. In the end the U.S. won, and Mexico eventually abandoned all claims to Texas and ceded a great deal of land (850,000 square miles!) to the U.S. This land included California, Nevada, and Utah, as well as parts of Arizona, New Mexico, and Wyoming.

Imagine:

What if Mexico had not lost the war, and never ceded land to the U.S.? What if all of that land still belonged to Mexico? Write a one-page essay predicting, under those circumstances, how life in the U.S. would be different now. No California means no Hollywood. Where would the movie stars live? No Disneyland. No Las Vegas. No Salt Lake City. How would this shift in history change the future of our country?

SECESSION

To secede or not to secede? That was the question facing southern states in 1861. Would they leave the Union and join a new country and government called the Confederate States of America? Or would they remain a part of the United States, governed under the new President Abraham Lincoln?

Many folks argued Texas should secede and leave the Union, even though the governor at the time, Sam Houston, desperately wanted Texas to remain part of the United States. Ultimately, he was outvoted by the citizens of Texas who preferred secession, and resigned because he would not sign an oath to be loyal to the Confederacy.

Just as Sam Houston whittled away on a piece of wood and pondered the right thing to do, many people consider the pros and cons before making a choice. In fact, when comparing choices, some say: "On one hand ...." then "On the other hand ..."

Imagine:

You are the governor of a southern state prior to the Civil War. Use the "On one hand ..." method to think through the choices and possible consequences of your decisions. List at least ten "On one hand ..." thoughts and after each, name an "On the other hand ..." alternate perspective. Finish the process with your final decision.

CIVIL WAR

The Civil War was a difficult time for America. Soldiers sometimes fought their own family members and friends in battle. Many lives and properties were destroyed, yet other lives were saved and the enslaved were set free. Individuals on both sides were forced to make a painful choice: would the end justify the means? In other words, would the desired outcome of the war be worth the devastation sure to be suffered by both the North and the South?

Readers frequently find a moral dilemma in novels and short stories. Sometimes right and wrong are not as clear as one might think. Write a short story about an individual living during the Civil War who faces a moral dilemma. Be sure to make the main character's thoughts clear to the reader. What are his/her choices? How will he/she decide the right thing to do?

The photograph you see above shows a soldier in a Confederate lookout tower at Bolivar Point in 1863 or 1864.

CONFLICT!

The history of our state ... our country ... our world is filled with stories of conflict. Wars. Natural disasters. Even individuals have conflict within themselves. What is the right thing to do? What is moral and good? Every fictional story has conflict as well. We learn from observing characters as they deal with problems and watch them solve issues within their heart and their environment. Perhaps we will someday be involved in a similar conflict or dilemma. We can hopefully look back and remember how a character, in a situation much like ours, solved a predicament successfully.

The Civil War was a time of great conflict. Conflict between people, governments, moral standards, and even the weather and disease. Write four paragraphs about the Civil War, fiction or non-fiction. Each paragraph should reflect one of these different conflicts: man versus man, man versus nature, man versus himself, and man versus society.

The photograph above shows non-commissioned officers, 19th Iowa Infantry - exchange prisoners from Camp Ford, Texas.

R.I.P.

Have you ever heard the term "irony?" Irony occurs in a situation when something seems contrary to what you expect ... and can cause an observer or reader to be amused at the result.

The gentleman you see here is Rip Ford. He commanded the Confederate forces in the final battle of the Civil War. Do you know what was ironic about that battle? The last battle of the Civil War was fought at Palmito Ranch near Brownsville, a month AFTER General Robert E. Lee surrendered. And in this case, the Confederate Army won the battle. So the last battle of the Civil War occurred in Texas, after the war was over, and the Confederacy won the battle. A strange but true ... and somewhat ironic story!

Now it's your turn to use irony in a story. You pick the setting, the characters, the plot. Just make sure to add an amusing bit of irony to your tale!

COWBOYS!

Some say "good fences make good neighbors." Why is that? Perhaps some believe it is better to keep our possessions separate from our neighbors to reduce conflict and confusion.

This was the case during the 1870s. Cowboys and ranchers needed wide open spaces to feed their cattle and drive their herds. But farmers wanted to protect their crops from the heavy, trampling hooves of these beasts. Farmers began to install barbed wire fences, sometimes leading to "wire cutting wars" between the farmer and the cowman.

Write a silly story from the perspective of a little calf. How does he feel about that barbed wire? What does he think when he sees it? Feels it? What does his owner say about the wire? What does the farmer say when he finds the little calf in his cabbage patch? Just for fun, use several examples of alliteration in your story.

Alliteration: when you use several words in a row with the same beginning sounds (crouching crazy calf!).

CATTLE DRIVE

Ah, the life of a cowboy! Wide open spaces, fresh air, beans, and biscuits.

Most cowboys would also tell you life on the trail wasn't all fun and games. He'd tell you about the good times, but just as easily tell you about both the boredom and the dangerous predicaments he encountered along the way.

Imagine:

*You are a cowboy (or cowgirl) on a cattle drive. Think about your day and all the interesting events that might happen on your journey. Then write a series of fortunate experiences followed by an unfortunate consequence. For example, you might write: "**Fortunately**, we were thirsty and arrived at a river. **Unfortunately**, that river was swarming with snakes!"*

Flashback to the Great Storm

Did you know Galveston's Great Storm of 1900 has long been considered the worst natural disaster in U.S. history? Over 6,000 people were killed during this devastating hurricane, not to mention the terrible destruction to homes and businesses. But those Galvestonians did not give up! They built a 17-foot tall seawall to protect their island from future storms, then actually raised the level of the island to help prevent flooding that might occur during the next hurricane.

Write a narrative memoir from the viewpoint of someone who survives the Great Storm. Instead of telling the story in chronological order, use flashbacks. In other words, start at the end of the story. Then have your character recall their experience through memories.

OIL!

Just months after the 1900 hurricane in Galveston, men were drilling for oil south of Beaumont on a small hill called Spindletop. At first, mud came out of the hole. Then a huge tower of mud, gas, and oil spewed up, up, up! Over 100,000 barrels of oil flowed every day. It took nine days to cap the well, but the news was out. More and more wells were drilled, and folks arrived from all over the country to work in and be a part of this new oil business. Still today, evidence of the ongoing oil and gas industry can be seen throughout the state. Wells, pumps, and refineries remind us of the importance of this natural resource.

Imagine:

You are a driller and observe the great gushing of oil at Spindletop. Using three similes, three metaphors, and three examples of personification in your story, describe the event from the standpoint of a very surprised and excited observer!

A simile is a figure of speech comparing two different things using the words "like" or "as." For example: "He is as cuddly as a teddy bear."

A metaphor also compares two different things, but doesn't use the words "like" or "as"; instead, the comparison only uses the word "is," but is not meant to be taken literally. For example: "He is a teddy bear."

Personification means giving an animal or nonliving object characteristics or abilities of a human. For example: "That piece of cake is calling my name!"

Women's Suffrage

It's hard to imagine. Our country existed for a long period of time, during which women could not vote! Eventually women's suffrage organizations across the country began to campaign for women's right to vote. Finally, in 1920, the 19th Amendment was ratified and all American women were given full voting rights.

Write a speech about voting. First, tell your audience whether or not you believe it is important for citizens to vote. Why or why not? At what age should people be allowed to vote? For what reasons should individuals not be allowed to vote? Do you plan to vote in the future, and why? Do individual votes make a difference? Do you agree with current voting laws? Why or why not?

DARK DAYS

The Great Depression and the Dust Bowl represent a very difficult time in America. Fortunes, savings, and businesses were lost after the Stock Market Crash of 1929. That meant homes and jobs were lost as well. At about the same time, many farms and crops were destroyed when drought and improper farming practices caused the top layer of soil to be exposed. This erosion, along with great winds, resulted in huge, choking dust storms. Many farms became useless as enormous clouds of dust would sometimes darken the skies for days. Families were often forced to leave their homes and look for work elsewhere.

Look for pictures taken during this time and you will have a better understanding of the tragedy many families faced. Write a free verse poem about the Dust Bowl.

Free verse poems do not have to rhyme, follow a specific tempo, or possess a certain number of lines. There are no rules; instead, focus on descriptive images, senses, and emotions. Paint a picture with words.

The little girl in the first photograph is the child of a migrant worker in a camp near Harlingen in 1939.
The second photo shows a Dust Bowl farm near Dalhart, Texas.

NAZIS IN THE GULF!

Many Texans are surprised to hear Nazi U-boats (submarines) were present in the Gulf of Mexico during World War II! These subs were sent to prevent ships carrying petroleum, and other supplies needed for the war effort, from leaving gulf ports and reaching their destinations. Surprisingly, fifty-six merchant ships and tankers were sunk by these German U-boats in the Gulf of Mexico between 1942-43, yet only one Nazi submarine in that area was destroyed.

Citizens living along the Gulf Coast took precautions. Some towns enforced nightly blackouts (everyone turned out their lights and covered windows), so the enemy subs could not see the profile of ships leaving port against the lights of the city. Some streets were closed along the seashore, and some cars even had little shutters on their headlights to make them harder to see at night.

Imagine:

You are alive during World War II. Your job is to inform citizens of potential dangers and recommend different ways to be cautious during this perilous time. Write a notice for the local newspaper, alerting citizens living near the coast about the presence of Nazi U-boats. Provide the readers with various methods to confuse the enemy and protect ships leaving port.

The Enemy is Near

While Nazi submarines trolled the waters along the Texas coast, a number of German, Italian, and Japanese soldiers were living on Texas soil! However, these soldiers were not a threat to Texas. They were being held in one of the prisoner of war camps located in our state. These prisoners were treated well and worked for local farms and factories, sometimes making new Texas friends and returning for a reunion after the war!

Imagine:

You have been hired by a major television streaming network to write a new series about a World War II POW (prisoner of war) imprisoned in a Texas camp. He develops a relationship with at least one Texan (a new buddy? A girlfriend?) and the friendship blossoms. Will your series end happily? Is it a drama or a comedy? Name the series, cast the characters with famous movie stars, and pick a location to film. Then write a short synopsis for each of the ten episodes. It's sure to win a major award!

Major Prisoner of War Camps in the United States (1944)

PROGRESS!

Texas has had a front-row seat to incredible human progress over the last few centuries. Railroads, telephones, the petroleum industry, medical research, computer technology ... even the space industry. Texas is the home of NASA's Johnson Space Center, Mission Control, and other important spaceflight businesses and activities.

Ask your parents about the changes in technology they have seen throughout their lifetime. Then it is your turn to predict. Write a short essay on what type of progress you believe you will see during the next thirty years. What will computers and phones look like in the future? What about airplanes and spaceflight? TVs and movies? Cars and other forms of transportation? Will life be better with the new technology or not? Explain.

Help Wanted

Texas government is designed very much like the federal (U.S.) government. Both governments are divided into three parts: the Executive, Legislative, and Judicial branches. The Legislative Branch (Congress, which is comprised of the Senate and House of Representatives) creates laws. The Executive Branch (the president/governor) is responsible for carrying out the laws properly and has the power to veto (disapprove) laws created by Congress (although Congress can override the veto). Finally, the Judicial Branch interprets the law and decides how to apply the laws to our country or state.

Write a "Help Wanted" ad for the positions of state governor, congressman/woman, and judge. Be sure to include the job description for each position and the type of personality you would hope to fill that position. Don't forget to mention who needs NOT apply!

Sing a Song of Congress

Duo. Pair. Deuce. Dyad. Twosome. Couple. Bicameral.

The Texas legislature is considered "bicameral" because there are two "chambers." These chambers (the Senate and the House of Representatives) work together to write and pass laws, appropriate education and other funds, and make important decisions about taxes and the economy. Thirty-one senators are elected for four-year terms, and the 150 members of the House of Representatives serve two-year terms. Both chambers meet in special big rooms located in the state capitol. They only meet and make decisions in regular session every other (odd-numbered) year, and for only up to 140 days. However, the governor can call an additional special session if an immediate need arises.

Pick a favorite nursery rhyme tune (like "Twinkle, Twinkle, Little Star" ***or*** "Bingo"***). Then write lyrics to that tune related to the activities and job description of the Texas legislature. Make sure to use your rhyming skills and try to make the syllables of the lyrics and rhythm match the tune.***

A BOOOO-TIFUL CAPITOL!

Have you ever visited our state capitol? Just imagine all of the important people who have walked those floors and the decisions made within those chambers. The history of the building makes this state treasure even more precious to its citizens. This particular building was completed in 1888, which means of course, many who served within those walls are no longer living. The high ceilings and tile floors create eerie and amazing echoes. It would be easy for one to become lost in the building's four hundred rooms, complete with huge, heavy doors and giant, brass door hinges. Life-sized statues of Sam Houston and Stephen F. Austin guard the entryway, keeping watch. Portraits of past presidents of the Republic and governors of the state encircle the rotunda, watching visitors, silently.

This sets the stage for a perfect ghost story! Write an eerie tale about a young person who is accidentally locked inside the capitol overnight. Use spine-tingling words to make your readers shiver with fright!

You're My Hero!

If you have completed a study of Texas history, then there is no doubt you have chosen at least a few Texas history heroes as your favorites.

Imagine:

You are given the ability to bring back three of your favorite heroes (at least two must be no longer living). Write down the questions you would ask each hero, followed by their responses. Perhaps they have questions for each other as well! Imagine you are preparing or taking the heroes out to dinner, so you'll have to also decide the setting of your conversation. And don't forget to bring a little gift for each hero. What would be an appropriate memento to give each of your guests? Be sure to ask them their opinions regarding today's technology, and find out—if they could remain in today's world—what type of job they would like to have in our modern society.

Short and Sweet!

Describe Texas in exactly fifty words. You might have to edit and adjust your writing to make the words fit. You will need to be as efficient as possible with your words, and as descriptive as you can in the process. Starting at the top left corner of the Panhandle, write your description along the inside perimeter of the Texas outline below.

A Place in History

Many books incorporate the element of time travel, and this book is no different!

Pick one event in Texas history you would like to observe in person. If you could travel back in time and participate in the event, what part would you play in the story? Describe the event in a short essay. Discuss why you selected this particular event, and explain why you find it interesting. Would you change anything about the event or its outcome?

How does this particular event fit in with the rest of the state history? If it hadn't occurred, do you think you would be sitting where you are today?

Photograph and Image Credits

Bluebonnet: User Ken/Flickr/CC BY 2.0. https://www.flickr.com
Spanish Flag: Rastrojo/Wikimedia Commons/CC BY 3.0.
https://commons.wikimedia.org/wiki/File:Flag_of_Castille_and_Le%C3%B3n.svg
French Flag: Zippanova/Wikimedia Commons/Public Domain.
https://commons.wikimedia.org/wiki/File:Pavillon_royal_de_France.svg
Mexico Flag: AlexCovarrubias/Wikimedia Commons/Public Domain.
https://commons.wikimedia.org/wiki/File:Flag_of_Mexico.svg
Lone Star Flag: Wikimedia Commons/Public Domain.
https://commons.wikimedia.org/w/index.php?curid=28388337
Confederate States of America Flag: Nicola Marschall/Wikimedia Commons/Public Domain. https://commons.wikimedia.org/wiki/File:Flag_of_the_Confederate_States_of_America_ (March_1861_%E2%80%93_May_1861).svg
United States of America Flag: MSGJ/Wikimedia Commons/Public Domain (implementation of the U.S. Code: Title 4, Chapter 1, Section 1 (1) (the United States Federal "Flag Law").
https://en.wikipedia.org/wiki/File:Flag_of_the_United_States
Mockingbird, Lightning Whelk Shell and Egg Case: photograph by author.
Buffalo: An American bison, common in the elk and bison prairie, closes his eyes while resting peacefully: courtesy of National Archives, Identifier 7722894, created by Dept of Transportation, Public Domain.
https://catalog.archives.gov/id/7722894
Alligator at Brazos Bend State Park: courtesy of photographer Jeanne Diarte.
Three Sisters Companion Planting Technigue. By Anna Juchnowicz - sent to OTRS, CC BY-SA 4.0,
https://commons.wikimedia.org/w/index.php?curid=69058558
Galveston Beach: photograph by author.
Coronado Sets Out to the North: painted by Frederic Remington. Wikimedia Commons/Public Domain.
https://commons, wikimedia.org/wiki/File:Coronado-Remington.jpg
Rene-Robert Cavelie, Sieur de La Salle: P.S.Burton/Wikimedia Commons/Public Domain.
https://commons.wikimedia.org/wiki/File:Cavelier_de_la_salle.jpg
La Salle's Expedition to Louisiana in 1684: painted by Theodore Gudin (1844). {{PD-1923}} The ship on the left is La Belle, in the middle is Le Joly, and L'Aimable, which has run aground, is to the far right. The ships are at the entrance to Matagorda Bay. AYER/Wikimedia Commons.
https://commons.wikimedia.org/wiki/File:LaSallesExpeditiontoLouisiana.JPG
Mission San José: photograph by author.
The Alamo: courtesy of photographer Grace Mercado-Marx.
Petticoat: CC0 1.0 Universal (CC0 1.0) Public Domain Dedication.
https://www.metmuseum.org/art/collection/search/159335 CC BY-SA 3.0
Moses Austin. http://www.bchm.org/Photos/p371.html, Public Domain, https://commons.wikimedia.org/w/index.php?curid=10355283 File:Moses Austin-P83-012-0012 enhanced 1.jpg. Created: 31 December 1820
Monument of Baron de Bastrop, Bastrop County, Texas. By HJKC (own work). File:Baron de Bastrop.png. CC BY-SA 3.0. Uploaded: 23 August 2014.
https://commons.wikimedia.org/wiki/File:Baron_de_Bastrop.png#/media/File:Baron_de_Bastrop.png.
Engraving of Stephen F. Austin: October 18, 1836, Early Texas Documents, Special Collections, University of Houston Libraries, accessed June 11, 2017. http://digital.lib.uh.edu/collection/earlytex/item/793/show/791
Dog trot Cabin and San Jacinto Monument: photograph by author.
Wood Engraving of Alamo, 1844: Courtesy Library of Congress.
Engraving of Sam Houston: approximately 1836, Early Texas Documents, Special Collections, University of Houston Libraries, accessed June 11, 2017. http://digital.lib.uh.edu/collection/earlytex/item/1105
General D. Antonio Lopez De Santa-Anna, president of the Republic of Mexico, c1847: courtesy of Library of Congress (LC-USZ62-21276). http://www.loc.gov/pictures/resource/cph.3a22346/
Color Potrait of Erastus "Deaf" Smith: painted by Thomas Jefferson Wright (1798-1846), approximately 1836, Early Texas Documents, Special Collections, University of Houston Libraries, accessed July 1, 2017.
http://digital.lib.uh.edu/collection/earlytex/item/1120

Come and Take It Flag: https://commons.wikimedia.org/wiki/File:Texas_Flag_Come_and_Take_It.svg#/media/File:Texas_Flag_Come_and_Take_It.svg. By Devin Cook (public domain) Feb 2008.
Washington-on-the-Brazos Independence Hall: photograph by author.
Mirabeau B. Lamar: Oldage07 (retouch and modifications)Wikimedia Commons, PD-US. http://commons.wikimedia.org/wiki/File:Mirabeaulamar_2.jpg
Burnet Flag: pumbaa80-own work/Public Domain. https://commons.wikimedia.org/w/index
Woodcut image of sailing ship: From *The Voyage of the Vega Round Asia and Europe Vol. 1*, written by A.E. Nordenskiold, published in 1881. Public Domain. http://www.reusableart.com/sailing-ship-01.html
Angelina Eberly Statue in Austin, Texas: photographed by author.
Black and White Beans. By artverau; courtesy of Pixabay.
https://pixabay.com/photos/beans-black-background-food-799943/
"The Republic of Texas is No More" - President Anson Jones, Annexation Ceremony, February 19, 1846: Identifier 0001103_0004, Places Collection, Prints and Photographs Collections. Archives and Information Services, Courtesy of Texas State Library and Archives Commission. http://tsl.access.preservica.com/file/sdb%3ADigitalFile%76ac00cle-e891-4b69-a9d3-51e57a60e739/
Texas Rangers, Company D, on Rio Grande, 1888-89: 1983/112 R-no number 1-1, Texas Department of Public Safety Photographs. Archives and Information Services Division, courtesy of Texas State Library and Archives Commission. https://tsl.access.preservica.com/file/sdb%3ADigitalFile%7C7f7f5405-7ea8-480b-b332-17af8c6ef102/
Hollywood:By Adrian104 - Own work, Public Domain, https://commons.wikimedia.org/w/index.php?curid=3464669
Soldier in Confederate Lookout Tower at Bolivar Point, c1863-64: Library of Congress (LC-DIG-stereo-1s01419). http://www.loc.gov/pictures/item/2005681147/
Non-commissioned officers, 19th Iowa Infantry, exchanged prisoners from Camp Ford, Texas: photographed at New Orleans on their arrival. United States, Non. (Beteween 1861-1869). Photograph. Retrieved from Library of Congress. https://www.loc.gov/item/cwp2003004635/PP/ (Accessed June 15, 2017)
RIP Ford: https://en.wikipedia.org/wiki/File:John-Salmon-Ford.jpg {{PD-US}}
Calf: photograph by author.
The Cow Boy: photographed by J.C.H. Grabill. Library of Congress (LC-USZ62-13227).
http://www.loc.gov/pictures/item/99613920/.
Help us to win the vote - Suffragist, "Mrs. Suffern," 1914: courtesy of Library of Congress (LC-USZ62-23622) George Grantham Bain Collection (Library of Congress) LC-B2-3022-10. http://www.loc.gov/pictures/item/97500240/
Texas Chief Gusher, c1919: courtesy of Library of Congress (LC-USZ62-39236).
http://www.loc.gov/pictures/item/2016648041/
Galveston Hurricane Aftermath: Galveston disaster, relief party working at Ave. P and Tremont St., c1900: courtesy of Library of Congress (LC-USZ62-71880). http://www.loc.gov/pictures/item/2003663540/
Child of Migrant Worker ironing in camp near Harlingen, Texas, 1939, Feb: photographed by Russell Lea, 1903-1986. LC-USF33-011999-M3. Courtesy of Library of Congress. https://www.loc.gov/item/fsa1997025214/PP/
Dust Bowl Farm near Dalhart, Texas: Dorothea Lange, photographer, June 1938. Courtesy of Library of Congress.
German Submarine U 3008 (30 August, 1946) Photograph from the Bureau of Ships Collection in the U.S. National Archives. Photo #: 19-N-95866. Public Domain. http://www.navsource.org/archives/08/08359.htm
Map of Major POW Camps in the U.S., June 1944By United States Army. http://www.sfasu.edu/heritagecenter/images/Scan_Pic0089_rdax_500x350.PNG, Public Domain, https://commons.wikimedia.org/w/index.php?curid=49262395
NASA Rocket: photograph by author.
Texas Capitol, Senate, & Rotunda Dome: photographed by author.
San Jacinto Reenactment and Alamo Cenotaph: photographed by author.
[Ta-Her-Ye-Qua-Hip or Horse-backs Camp; 4 comanches in front of wigwam, Fort Sill, Indian Territory]: ca. 1873. Photograph. Retrieved from the Library of Congress. https://www.loc.gov/item/2016649448/
Juan Seguín Memorial statue in Seguín, Tx: Amboo who?/Flickr (CC BY-SA 2.0) - crop/bw.
https://www.flickr.com/photos/aboo213/34688464521/in/photolist-URirYv-q58RHB-qYUpTp-7PnEyN-7PiHED-oRzqwo-quBjRX-quBmL8-qKA6ft
Texas Outline: Shutterstock By skvoor ID: 8086282
Social Media Text Graphic: Shutterstock. By grebeshkovmaxim. ID: 1066870904.
Social Media Cell Phone Graphic: Shutterstock. By thebigland. ID: 559066345.
Cover Image: Shutterstock By Seita ID: 168881672

Made in the USA
Columbia, SC
24 March 2019